Paddle Perch Climb

Bird Feet Are Neat

Written and Illustrated by Laurie Ellen Angus

Dawn Publications

To my fledgling ornithologist husband, Richard. —LA

Acknowledgments

Special thanks to my editor, Carol, whose support and guidance has been
indispensable in making this book the best it can be. — LA

The publisher wishes to thank Louisa Malnor, 13 years old,
for creating the detailed pen and ink bird feet drawings
that appear in "Explore More for Kids"

Library of Congress Cataloging-in-Publication Data

Names: Angus, Laurie, author, illustrator.
Title: Paddle perch climb: bird feet are neat / written and illustrated by
Laurie Ellen Angus.
Description: First edition. | Nevada City, CA: Dawn Publications, [2018] |
Includes bibliographical references.
Identifiers: LCCN 2017018745| ISBN 9781584696131 (hardcover) | ISBN
9781584696148 (pbk.)
Subjects: LCSH: Birds--Juvenile literature. | Foot--Juvenile literature.
Classification: LCC QL676.2 .A57 2018 | DDC 598--dc23 LC record
available at https://lccn.loc.gov/2017018745

Book design and computer production by
Patty Arnold, *Menagerie Design & Publishing*

Manufactured by Regent Publishing Services, Hong Kong
Printed January, 2018, in ShenZhen, Guangdong, China

10 9 8 7 6 5 4 3 2 1
First Edition

Dawn Publications

12402 Bitney Springs Road
Nevada City, CA 95959
800-545-7475
www.dawnpub.com

If you were a hungry bird, how could you use your feet to eat?

If you had **webbing** between your toes, you could...

Paddle like a swan to dabble for pond plants.

Watch out for the fox!

If you had long
slender legs and toes,
you could...

Wade like a heron to sneak up on a school of fish.

Be careful of the bobcat!

If you had **strong feet and legs**,
you could...

Run like a
roadrunner to
snag a lizard for lunch.

Look out! A coyote!

If you had
**toes with claws
that can cling,**
you could...

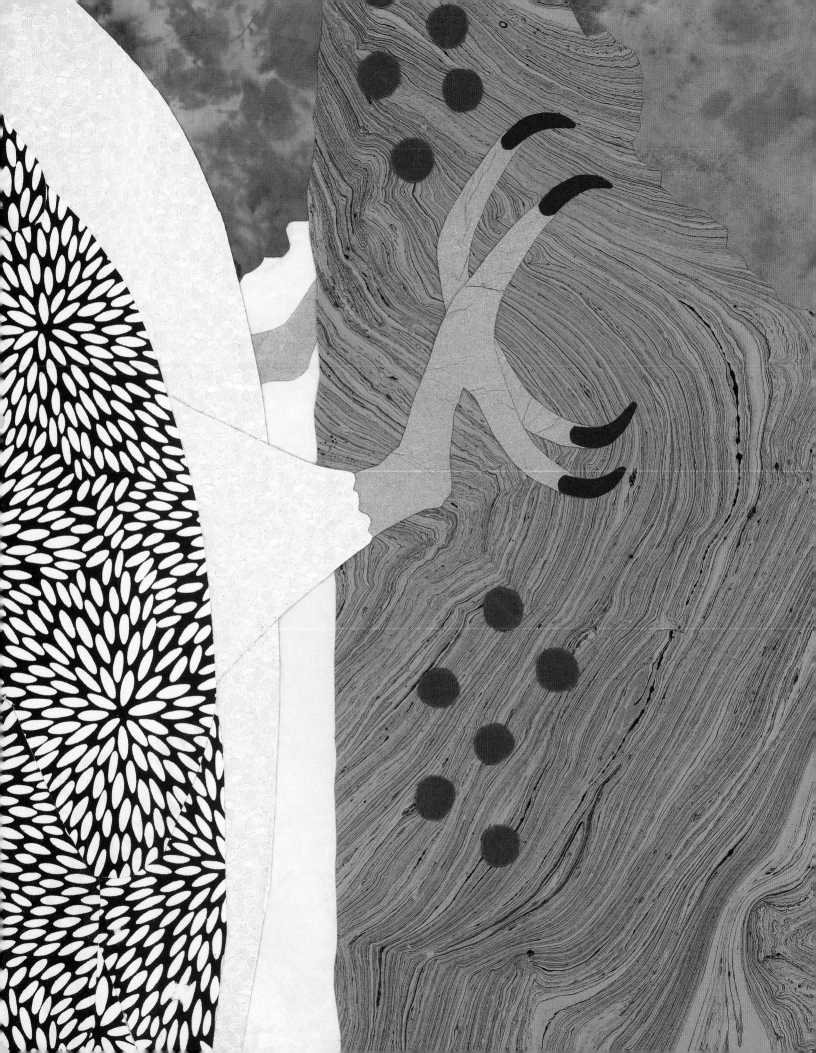

Climb like a woodpecker to peck for grubs.

Uh, oh! Keep an eye on the snake!

If you had **small flexible toes,**
you could...

Perch like a cardinal
to pick some berries.

Or, you could...

Scratch like a towhee
to search for bugs.

Beware! A hawk!

If you had
powerful feet with sharp talons,
you could...

Grasp like an owl to grab a mouse.

Keep your owlets safe!

If you were a hungry bird, there are many ways to use your feet to eat.

Bird Feet Are REALLY Neat

Bird feet come in many amazing shapes and sizes. You can learn a lot about a bird just by looking at its feet. The size, shape, and type of feet and legs give you important clues about where it lives, what it eats, and how it moves.

Let's Go Swimming—Mute Swans are waterfowl. They live in ponds, rivers, and lakes. Waterfowl have flat webbing between their toes that helps them *paddle* through the water. Swans mainly eat water plants. They also eat insects, tadpoles, and snails. Geese and ducks are also waterfowl.

Fun Foot Fact:

Because swans have short legs that are located toward the back of their big bodies, they waddle when they walk on land.

Gone Fishing—Great Blue Herons are wading birds. Wading birds have long toes that keep them from sinking into soft mud. They live in wetlands. Herons also have long legs. They can *wade* in water up to their bellies without getting their feathers wet. Herons eat fish, insects, and amphibians. Some other wading birds are cranes, rails, and jacanas.

Fun Foot Fact:

The Great Blue Heron is four feet tall, with long legs and toes. It looks down from high above the water to spot a meal. It spears its prey and then swallows it in one big gulp.

Born to Run—A Greater Roadrunner is a type of cuckoo. Roadrunners have strong legs and feet. They can *run* quickly and easily over rocks and sand to catch fast-running desert animals. Their top speed is about 20 miles per hour (32 km per hour). Roadrunners can eat venomous lizards and scorpions. They'll eat a rattlesnake, too. But first they kill it by beating it against a rock.

Fun Foot Fact:

Roadrunner feet make X-shaped tracks. Native American legends say that these tracks disguise which way a roadrunner is going.

Going Up—Red-bellied Woodpeckers are a type of climbing bird. Woodpeckers have two toes pointing forward and two pointing back. Woodpeckers *climb* up trees pecking for grubs under tree bark.

Fun Foot Fact:

Their back toes keep them from falling backwards while they climb and peck. They also have sharp claws that help them hold on tightly.

Out on a Limb—Northern Cardinals are a type of perching bird. Perching birds are also called song birds. Their slender, flexible toes allow them to grip tightly when they *perch* on branches and twigs. They have four toes—three toes pointing forward and one back. Like many birds, male Cardinals are more brightly colored (red) than females (brown).

Fun Foot Fact:

When a perching bird lands, it bends it legs. This causes a tendon to tighten the bird's feet around the branch. The bird stays locked in place until it stands up. Then the tendon relaxes, the toes loosen their grip, and the bird can fly away.

Hippity Hop—Spotted Towhees live in shrubs and bushes. They spend most of their time on the ground *scratching* to look for seeds and bugs.

Fun Foot Fact:

To find food in the leaves, Towhees quickly hop backwards and forwards with both feet at the same time. This is called a "two-footed hop" or a "double scratch." You might hear them rustling in dry leaves beneath bushes.

Get a Grip—A Great Horned Owl is a bird of prey. A bird of prey is also called a raptor. Owls live in many different habitats. Most are nocturnal, which means they are most active at night. Great Horned Owls swoop down to the ground to *grasp* their prey. They eat rodents, rabbits, and just about any animal they can kill and carry away.

Fun Foot Fact:

Owls have the strongest grip of all raptors. They have three toes pointing forward and one pointing backward. But they can swivel one of their forward-pointing toes to the back. This gives them a good grip when catching prey or perching.

The Bird That Inspired This Book

While watching the usual assortment of birds perched on our feeder one morning, a brilliantly colored Red-bellied Woodpecker unexpectedly flew down from a tree, eager to join the feast. Because woodpeckers' feet are designed to cling to vertical surfaces, I was curious to see if it could land on the feeder's horizontal bar. It tried again and again. But despite all of its efforts, it just wasn't able to grasp tightly enough. Finally, it flew back to the tree; and clinging tightly to the trunk, it pecked under the tree bark for grubs.

After watching this woodpecker, I became inspired to share a story about how birds' feet have adapted to help them survive. Of course, I included a Red-bellied Woodpecker in the book! And thanks to my husband, who installed a vertical feeder, the woodpecker is now able to enjoy the same delicious food as the perching birds.

About the artwork: Paper collage is my favorite way to make pictures, and I love bold shapes and lots of color! I also like to make some characters really large, which makes them feel up close and almost touchable.

Adaptations—Form and Function

Bird feet are uniquely specialized to survive in a particular habitat—the form is perfectly suited to its function. But feet aren't a bird's only adaptation. A bird's bill, also called a beak, is another important feature that helps a bird to survive. Look at the illustrations and notice each bird's beak.

Design a Bird—Review and discuss the information in the following chart with your children. (This chart is also available as a download at dawnpub.com/activity) Have children work

in pairs or small groups to choose a habitat and design a bird that is adapted for living there. The bird can be imaginary, but the feet and beak should be accurate for their habitat and the food the bird eats. Children may draw a picture or create a 3-D model using materials such as foam balls, construction paper, felt, craft sticks, toothpicks, cardboard, paint, etc. Have children display their birds to the whole class and ask others to guess the habitat.

BIRD	HABITAT	FEET	BEAK
Swans	Ponds, lakes, rivers	Webbed feet for paddling	Flat bill with serrated edges to strain plants and insects out of the water
Herons	Wetlands	Long legs and toes for wading	Spear-like bill to strike and grab fish, frogs, and other aquatic animals
Roadrunners	Desert	Agile feet and muscular legs for running	Pointed bill to catch insects, snakes, and small animals
Woodpeckers	Forest	Toes with claws that cling for climbing tree trunks	Chisel-like beak to drill into trees for insects
Cardinals	Trees, bushes	Small, flexible toes for perching	Thick, conical beak to break open seeds. Also eats insects and berries
Towhees	Bushes, shrubs	Toes that can perch and scratch	Thick, conical beak to break open seeds. Also eats insects
Owls	Wide variety	Strong feet and sharp talons for grasping prey	Sharp, hooked beak to tear up prey

Look Out!

While birds are eating, they need to be careful not to get eaten. The animals hiding in some of the illustrations, including a fox, bobcat, coyote, and hawk, are just a few of the many predators that eat birds. Some birds, snakes, and other animals will raid nests, eating eggs and nestlings.

Create Food Chains: Choose one of the habitats from the story and create a food chain or food web that includes one of the predators. You may use a coat hanger and yarn to make a mobile with the main predator at the top and some of the animals it eats hanging below it. Plants would hang at the bottom because they are the basis for most food chains.

I Wonder . . .

What makes a bird a bird?
All birds share these characteristics:

- Feathers—Birds are the only living animal to have feathers.

- Two wings—Not all birds use their wings to fly.

- Two legs and two feet—And now you know the different types!

- A bill, also called a beak—The shape is adapted to what the bird eats.

- Lay eggs—The ostrich lays the largest egg—over 3 pounds (1.36 kilograms).

- Are warm-blooded—Like mammals, birds maintain a steady body temperature.

Most birders and scientists estimate that there are about 10,000 species of birds in the world. Perching birds are the largest category of birds—about 5,000 species.

Get Curious: Asking questions is an important part of scientific discovery. Help children develop this skill by brainstorming questions about birds, for example: Do bird feet get cold in winter? Why don't baby birds fall out of the nest? How do birds sleep? Use the resources under "More Fun with Birds" to find the answers.

Bird Watching Tips

Use the following bird watching tips to introduce children to the wonderful world of birds at home or school. And remember, you don't have to identify every bird you see. Just enjoy watching them!

- Start close to home. Begin by getting to know the birds in your backyard or school grounds.

- Attract birds by putting up a feeder or setting up a bird bath.

- Listen! Birds have both songs and calls that will tell you where they are.

- Birds may be startled by noise and movement. Be patient if they fly away—they will probably return if you sit quietly for a few moments.

- Use binoculars to see birds more clearly. A bird field guide will help you identify the birds you see.

- When trying to identify a bird, first notice its general size and shape. Then look for special colors and markings.

More Fun with Birds

Find information, projects, birding tips, and curriculum:

National Audubon Society, dedicated to education and conservation —audubon.org

Cornell Lab of Ornithology, offers numerous resources including All About Birds, Project Feeder Watch, and Bird Sleuth—birds.cornell.edu

Bird Watcher's Digest, informative and entertaining—birdwatchersdigest.com

Great Backyard Bird Count, a citizen science project for all ages—gbbc.birdcount.org

Don't Miss It! There are many useful resources online for most of Dawn's books, including activities and standards-based lesson plans. Scan this code to go directly to activities for this book, or go to www.dawnpub.com and click on "Activities" for this and other books.

Laurie Ellen Angus lives alongside a creek in a wooded area, which gives her many opportunities to observe nature up close and personal. Her backyard is a playground for many wild creatures, as well as a diverse assortment of birds, including hawks, hummingbirds, and egrets. One of Laurie's favorites, a screech owl she named Nascha, also makes its home nearby, trilling softly at night for its mate. Through her books, Laurie endeavors to spark children's curiosity about the incredible diversity of life on our planet and to become avid nature lovers and explorers. Laurie attended Parson's School of Design in NYC. This is her second book for Dawn Publications. She is also the author and illustrator of *Octopus Escapes Again!*

Also Written and Illustrated by Laurie Angus

Octopus Escapes Again!—Swim along with Octopus as she leaves the safety of her den to search for food. Will she eat? Or will she be eaten? She outwits dangerous enemies by using a dazzling display of defenses—clouds of ink, jet propulsion, camouflage, and more!

More Nature Appreciation Books by Dawn Publications

The BLUES Go Birding series—Follow five intrepid blue birds as they discover a remarkable variety of birds all across America and around the world.

Noisy Bird Sing-Along—Every kind of bird has its very own kind of sound. You can tell who they are without even opening your eyes and what fun to sing along!

There's a Bug on My Book—Take this book outside and plop down on the grass. All sorts of creatures will join you. Tilt, tap, or jiggle the book to discover the fascinating way each animal moves.

Wonderful Nature, Wonderful You—Nature can be a great teacher. Its gentle messages encourage children, and all of us, to be the best we can be—naturally!

Daytime Nighttime, All Through the Year—Delightful rhymes depict two animals for each month, one active during the day and one busy at night.

Tall Tall Tree—Take a peek at some of the animals that make their home in a tall, tall, tree—a magnificent coast redwood. Rhyming verses and a 1–10 counting scheme make this a real page-turner.

A Moon of My Own—Follow an adventurous young girl as she discovers natural beauty and man made wonders, accompanied by her faithful companion—the Moon.

Dawn Publications is dedicated to inspiring in children a deeper understanding and appreciation for all life on Earth. You can browse through our titles, download resources for teachers, and order at www.dawnpub.com or call 800-545-7475.